# Greatest Ever

# One Pot

## The All Time Top 20 Greatest Recipes

*p*

This is a Parragon Book
This edition published in 2002

Parragon
Queen Street House
4 Queen Street
Bath BA1 1HE, UK

ISBN: 0-75259-290-4

Printed in China

**NOTE**

This book uses metric and imperial measurements. Follow the same
units of measurement throughout; do not mix metric and imperial.
All spoon measurements are level: teaspoons are assumed to be 5 ml,
and tablespoons are assumed to be 15 ml. Unless otherwise stated,
milk is assumed to be full fat, eggs and individual vegetables such as
potatoes are medium, and pepper is freshly ground black pepper.

The times given for each recipe are an approximate guide only
because the preparation times may differ according to the techniques
used by different people and the cooking times may vary as a result
of the type of oven used. The preparation times include marinating,
chilling and freezing times, where appropriate.

Recipes using raw or very lightly cooked eggs should be
avoided by infants, the elderly, pregnant women, convalescents,
and anyone suffering from an illness.

# CONTENTS

# INTRODUCTION

*One-pot dishes are simply perfect for midweek family meals, weekend lunches and informal supper parties – no mess, no fuss, just an appetizing aroma wafting gently from a quietly bubbling pan or casserole in a tidy kitchen. Pour a glass of wine and put your feet up, while dinner takes care of itself. Afterwards, when the plates are empty and appetites are fully satisfied, there is hardly any washing up to do. What could be easier?*

The mere phrase 'one-pot meals' evokes images of rich, comforting, hearty stews and casseroles, and these are certainly firm favourites in most families. It would be hard to think of anything more welcome on a chilly winter's evening than a steaming plate of Beef & Potato Goulash or Savoury Hot Pot.

However, one-pot cooking has more than this to offer, and the 20 recipes in this book include dishes for every time of year and for all occasions. Try Easy Cheese Risotto for a family weekend lunch, Mediterranean Chicken & Peppers for an al fresco supper, or impress your guests with a flamboyant Spanish Paella. Fabulous vegetarian dishes include an exotic Vegetable Jambalaya and the substantial Casseroled Beans & Penne with Herbs – both of which will appeal equally to meat-eaters.

peppers

Virtually every cuisine in the world includes one-pot dishes, not just because they are easy, but because while they are cooking, the flavours of the various ingredients blend into delicious, mouth-watering combinations.

The recipes in this book span an international spectrum, from Brittany to Louisiana and from Italy to Azerbaijan. Ingredients are as varied as the countries that inspired the recipes – meat, poultry, fish, sausages, rice, pasta and a colourful array of vegetables. There is a dish to suit everyone, and a huge variety of delicious flavours, from spicy Cajun Chicken Gumbo to succulent Italian Sausage Casserole.

sausages

aubergines

potatoes

broccoli

carrots

pumpkin

**Above:** Slow-cooked one-pot meals allow time for the flavours of different foods to develop. The freshest ingredients will always give the best results.

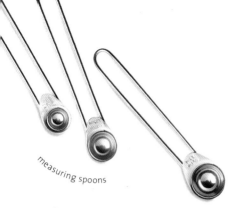

measuring spoons

*For successful one-pot cooking, high-quality cookware is essential. It is worth spending the extra money on solid, well-made pans, which will last longer and cook more efficiently than cheaper, flimsy ones.*

# EQUIPMENT

## Saucepans

milkpan

saucepan

saucepan with lid

frying pan

You will need a range of saucepans in different sizes for stews, risottos and pilafs. They need to be large enough to hold all the ingredients comfortably – remember that, in the case of risotto, the rice will swell to about three times its original size – and you will probably also need to allow room for stirring during cooking without splashing yourself or the hob.

If a pan is too small, the ingredients of a stew will be too tightly packed and will not cook properly. The results will be disappointingly tough and underdone. Equally, if a pan is too large, too much liquid will evaporate and the dish will dry out.

Choose pans with a heavy base, which will heat evenly and maintain a steady temperature. Large saucepans are easier and safer to lift – especially when full of a simmering stew – if there are two handles. It is important that the handles are securely attached and cannot work loose. Heatproof handles are safer than metal ones, which conduct heat.

The pans also require tight-fitting lids, to seal in the flavour. Glass lids are ideal, as you can check on the progress of the dish without disturbing the seal that forms during cooking.

## Oven dishes

Ovenproof dishes are required for casseroles and bakes, again in a range of sizes. It is useful to have at least one round and one rectangular dish, and one round and one oval casserole.

Flameproof casseroles are particularly useful for one-pot dishes, as they can be used both on the hob and in the oven. They are available in a wide range of attractive designs, so your one-pot meal can go straight from the oven to the table, dispensing with the need for a separate serving dish.

perforated spoon

wooden spoons

knives

ladle

## Frying pans

A large, heavy-based frying pan is useful for dishes such as paella. Pans with curved sides prevent food from sticking round the edges of the base during cooking.

Modern, fused non-stick coatings are more reliable than the older types, although more expensive. They can withstand higher temperatures and are quite satisfactory for browning meat. The older type of non-stick coating is not so good for browning and is more easily damaged by careless handling. Alternatively, use a cast iron pan.

## Other equipment

You will probably have much of the other equipment you need in your kitchen already, such as chopping boards, a grater, a set of knives, wooden and perforated spoons, a heatproof measuring jug and measuring spoons.

You will need at least two cook's knives. A paring knife with a short, pointed blade is useful for peeling and trimming vegetables and fruit. A chopping knife with a heavy, wide blade about 18–20 cm/7–8 inches long is ideal for chopping vegetables, meat and herbs. For your safety, it is important to use the right size of knife for the job and to keep it sharp. Most injuries are caused by a blunt knife slipping.

A swivel-blade vegetable peeler will enable you to peel vegetables very thinly and retain the nutrients that are concentrated directly under the skin. It is also useful for shaving hard cheese, such as Parmesan, to use as a garnish. Finally, a ladle is essential for making risottos and useful for serving stews. Choose one with a heatproof handle and a pouring lip.

measuring jug

scales

ovenproof casserole dish

chopping boards

When it comes to planning a family meal or dinner party, you will need to think about what you can serve to complement your one-pot dish. Try to keep things simple – choose accompaniments and desserts that will not require a great deal of preparation, so that the entire meal is quick and easy to put together.

# MAKING A MEAL OF IT

There are many tasty extras to serve with one-pot dishes that do not need any cooking, but which can turn an ordinary supper into a feast. Basing a meal around any of the one-pot recipes in this book and using just a little imagination when it comes to accompaniments makes entertaining almost effortless and very enjoyable.

raspberries

strawberries

bananas

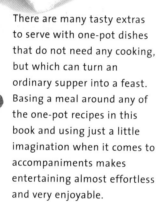

cherries

pineapple

## Breads

The range of breads available in supermarkets is extensive nowadays. French sticks have always been popular, go well with most dishes and would be the perfect choice for mopping up the delicious juices of Cotriade. Italian breads, such as ciabatta and focaccia – with or without extra flavourings such as olives or sun-dried tomatoes – are the perfect companions for risottos and other Mediterranean dishes. The firm texture of soda bread, sourdough and rustic breads makes them ideal for serving with hearty stews and casseroles, while a basket of assorted rolls – brown and white, plain and knotted, and a few topped with seeds – is an attractive addition to any dinner table.

## Salads

You can serve salads as an accompaniment to a one-pot dish, as an appetizer beforehand or as a French-

spinach

style palate cleanser afterwards. As well as familiar salad leaves, such as cos, butterhead and iceberg lettuce, most supermarkets stock convenient packs of ready-prepared, more exotic leaves, such as rocket, radicchio, escarole, lollo rosso, lollo bianco, oak-leaf, tatsoi, lamb's lettuce and mizuna. You can also make delicious salads with baby spinach, and adding fresh herbs, such as basil, coriander or mint, makes all leafy salads a little more special.

Many other types of salad are almost as quick and easy to prepare. Home-made coleslaw is a real treat and if you use different types of cabbage, it looks colourful. Try mixing three kinds of drained canned beans with chopped raw onion and a vinaigrette for a substantial accompaniment. Tomato and onion is a classic salad, and combining a mixture of sprouted seeds, apple and cucumber with a herb dressing takes only minutes.

## Desserts

Round off the meal with a no-cook dessert. Fresh seasonal fruit is always welcome, especially following a spicy or hearty main course. Individual bowls of ripe cherries set on beds of ice cubes is simplicity itself, but pretty enough to serve to dinner guests. A basket of summer fruits, such as nectarines, figs, apricots and plums, is colourful, and who can resist strawberries or raspberries, swimming in cream? A fresh fruit salad is hardly any more effort and you can add an extra touch with a splash of wine or a favourite liqueur.

Gâteaux and other elegant pâtisserie are widely available from supermarkets and specialist shops. On the Continent, especially in France and Italy, these are rarely home-made, so don't feel you are cheating your guests. Ice cream and sorbets are lovely in the summer months, and you can serve them on their own, or with fruit or attractive biscuits.

Finally, don't forget that a cheeseboard is a delicious way to end a meal. Offer three or four different types of cheese – creamy, blue, hard and semi-hard, for example – with a basket of crackers and crispbread and fresh butter. Alternatively, serve slices of Brie with seedless grapes.

coriander

onions

spring onions

tomatoes

pears

# CREAMY CHICKEN
# & POTATO CASSEROLE

>Serves 4   >Preparation time: 10 minutes   >Cooking time: 1 hour 40 minutes

## INGREDIENTS

2 tbsp vegetable oil

4 chicken portions, about 225 g/8 oz each

2 leeks, sliced

1 garlic clove, crushed

55 g/2 oz plain flour

850 ml/1½ pints chicken stock

300 ml/10 fl oz dry white wine

125 g/4½ oz baby carrots, halved lengthways

125 g/4½ oz baby corn cobs, halved lengthways

450 g/1 lb small new potatoes

1 bouquet garni

150 ml/5 fl oz double cream

salt and pepper

rice or broccoli, to serve

## METHOD

**1** Heat the oil in a large frying pan. Fry the chicken portions for 10 minutes, turning until browned all over. Transfer the chicken to a casserole dish using a perforated spoon.

**2** Add the leek and garlic to the frying pan and fry for 2–3 minutes, stirring. Stir in the flour and cook for another minute. Remove the frying pan from the heat and stir in the stock and wine. Season well.

**3** Return the pan to the heat and bring the mixture slowly to the boil. Stir in the carrots, corn cobs, potatoes and bouquet garni.

**4** Transfer the mixture to the casserole. Cover and cook in a preheated oven, 180°C/350°F/Gas Mark 4, for about 1 hour.

**5** Remove the casserole from the oven and stir in the cream. Return the casserole to the oven uncovered, and cook for another 15 minutes. Remove the bouquet garni and discard it. Taste and adjust the seasoning, if necessary, and serve the casserole with plain rice or fresh vegetables, such as broccoli.

# RUSTIC CHICKEN & ORANGE POT

>Serves 4   >Preparation time: 5 minutes   >Cooking time: 1 hour

## INGREDIENTS

8 skinless chicken drumsticks

1 tbsp wholemeal flour

1 tbsp olive oil

2 red onions

1 garlic clove, crushed

1 tsp fennel seeds

1 bay leaf

finely grated rind and juice of 1 small orange

400 g/14 oz canned chopped tomatoes

400 g/14 oz canned cannellini or flageolet beans, drained

salt and pepper

### TOPPING

3 thick slices wholemeal bread, crusts removed

2 tsp olive oil

## METHOD

**1** Toss the chicken in the flour to coat evenly. Heat the oil in a non-stick pan. Add the chicken and cook over a fairly high heat, turning frequently, until golden brown. Transfer to a large casserole.

**2** Slice the red onions into thin wedges. Add to the pan and cook over a medium heat for a few minutes until lightly browned. Stir in the garlic, then add the onions and garlic to the casserole dish.

**3** Add the fennel seeds, bay leaf, orange rind and juice, tomatoes and cannellini or flageolet beans and season to taste.

**4** Cover tightly and cook in a preheated oven, 190°C/375°F/Gas Mark 5, for 30–35 minutes until the chicken juices run clear when the meat is pierced with a skewer.

**5** To make the topping, cut the bread into small dice and toss in the oil. Remove the lid from the casserole and sprinkle the bread on top of the chicken. Bake for a further 15–20 minutes until the bread is golden and crisp. Serve hot straight from the casserole.

# EASY CHEESE RISOTTO

>Serves 4–6   >Preparation time: 5 minutes   >Cooking time: 30–35 minutes

## INGREDIENTS

4–5 tbsp unsalted butter

1 onion, finely chopped

300 g/10½ oz arborio or carnaroli rice

125 ml/4 fl oz dry white vermouth or white wine

1.2 litres/2 pints chicken or vegetable stock, simmering

85 g/3 oz freshly grated Parmesan cheese, plus extra for sprinkling

salt and pepper

## METHOD

**1** Heat about 2 tablespoons of the butter in a large heavy-based saucepan over a medium heat. Add the onion and cook for 2 minutes, or until just beginning to soften. Add the rice and cook for 2 minutes, stirring frequently, until translucent and well coated with the butter.

**2** Pour in the vermouth: it will bubble and steam rapidly and evaporate almost immediately. Add a ladleful of the simmering stock and cook, stirring constantly, until the stock is absorbed.

**3** Continue adding the stock about half a ladleful at a time, allowing each addition to be absorbed by the rice before adding the next. This should take about 20–25 minutes. The finished risotto should have a creamy consistency and the cooked rice grains should be tender, but still firm to the bite.

**4** Remove the pan from the heat and stir the remaining butter and the grated Parmesan cheese into the risotto. Season with salt and a little pepper, to taste. Cover, leave to stand for about 1 minute, then serve hot with extra grated Parmesan for sprinkling.

# SAVOURY HOT POT

›Serves 4  ›Preparation time: 15 minutes  ›Cooking time: 2 hours

## INGREDIENTS

8 middle neck lean lamb chops, neck of lamb
or any lean stewing lamb

1–2 garlic cloves, crushed

2 lambs' kidneys, optional

1 large onion, thinly sliced

1 leek, sliced

2–3 carrots, sliced

1 tsp chopped fresh tarragon or sage, or ½ tsp
dried tarragon or sage

1 kg/2 lb 4 oz potatoes, thinly sliced

300 ml/10 fl oz lamb stock

2 tbsp margarine, melted, or 1 tbsp vegetable
oil

salt and pepper

chopped fresh parsley, to garnish

## METHOD

**1** Trim any excess fat from the lamb, season
well and arrange in a large ovenproof
casserole. Sprinkle with the garlic.

**2** If using kidneys, remove the skin, halve and
cut out the cores. Chop into small pieces and
sprinkle them over the lamb.

**3** Place the vegetables over the lamb, allowing
the pieces to slip in between the meat, then
sprinkle with the herbs.

**4** Arrange the potato slices on top of the meat
and vegetables, in an overlapping pattern.

**5** Bring the stock to the boil, season to taste,
then pour over the casserole.

**6** Brush the potatoes with the melted
margarine or oil, cover and cook in a preheated
oven, 180°C/350°F/Gas Mark 4, for 1½ hours.

**7** Remove the cover from the casserole,
increase the temperature to 220°C/425°F/Gas
Mark 7 and return to the oven for about
30 minutes until the potatoes are browned.

**8** Garnish the hot pot with chopped fresh
parsley and serve hot.

# CAJUN CHICKEN GUMBO

›Serves 2 ›Preparation time: 5 minutes ›Cooking time: 25 minutes

## INGREDIENTS

1 tbsp sunflower oil

4 chicken thighs

1 small onion, diced

2 celery sticks, diced

1 small green pepper, deseeded and diced

85 g/3 oz long-grain rice

300 ml/10 fl oz chicken stock

1 small red chilli

225 g/8 oz okra

1 tbsp tomato purée

salt and pepper

## METHOD

**1** Heat the oil in a wide pan and fry the chicken until golden. Remove the chicken from the pan.

**2** Put the onion, celery and pepper in the pan and fry for 1 minute. Pour off any excess oil.

**3** Add the rice and fry, stirring, for a further minute. Add the chicken stock and bring to the boil. Thinly slice the red chilli and trim the okra, and stir in to the gumbo with the tomato purée. Season to taste with salt and pepper.

**4** Return the chicken to the pan and stir. Cover tightly and simmer gently for 15 minutes, or until the rice is tender, the chicken is thoroughly cooked and the liquid absorbed. Stir occasionally and if it becomes too dry, add a little extra stock.

# SPANISH PAELLA

>Serves 4   >Preparation time: 5 minutes   >Cooking time: 55 minutes

## INGREDIENTS

125 ml/4 fl oz olive oil

1.5 kg/3 lb 5 oz chicken, cut into eight pieces

350 g/12 oz chorizo sausage, cut into
1-cm/½-inch pieces

115 g/4 oz cured ham, chopped

2 onions, finely chopped

2 red peppers, deseeded and cut into 2.5-cm/
1-inch pieces

4–6 garlic cloves

750 g/1 lb 10 oz short-grain Spanish rice or
Italian arborio rice

2 bay leaves

1 tsp dried thyme

1 tsp saffron threads, lightly crushed

225 ml/8 fl oz dry white wine

1.5 litres/2¾ pints chicken stock

115 g/4 oz fresh shelled or defrosted
frozen peas

450 g/1 lb medium uncooked prawns

8 raw king prawns, in shells

16 clams, very well scrubbed

16 mussels, very well scrubbed

4 tbsp chopped fresh flat-leaved parsley

salt and pepper

## METHOD

**1** Heat half the oil in a 46-cm/18-inch paella pan over a medium-high heat. Add the chicken and fry, turning, until golden. Remove from the pan and set aside. Add the chorizo and ham to the pan and cook for 7 minutes, stirring occasionally, until crisp. Remove and set aside.

**2** Add the onions to the pan. Cook until soft. Add the peppers and garlic, cook until beginning to soften. Remove and set aside.

**3** Add the remaining oil to the pan. Stir in the rice until coated. Add the bay leaves, thyme and saffron and stir. Pour in the wine, bubble, then add the stock, stirring and scraping the bottom of the pan. Bring to the boil, stirring.

**4** Gently stir in the cooked vegetables and the chorizo, ham and chicken. Reduce the heat and cook for 10 minutes, stirring occasionally.

**5** Add the peas and prawns, cook for 5 minutes, then push the clams and mussels into the rice. Cover, cook over a very low heat for 5 minutes until the shellfish open, then discard any unopened clams or mussels. Season to taste.

**6** Remove from the heat, and stand, covered, for 5 minutes. Sprinkle with parsley and serve.

# CASSEROLED BEANS & PENNE WITH HERBS

>Serves 4  >Preparation time: 10 minutes  >Cooking time: 3½ hours

## INGREDIENTS

225 g/8 oz dried haricot beans, soaked
overnight and drained

225 g/8 oz dried penne

6 tbsp olive oil

850 ml/1½ pints vegetable stock

2 large onions, sliced

2 garlic cloves, chopped

2 bay leaves

1 tsp dried oregano

1 tsp dried thyme

5 tbsp red wine

2 tbsp tomato purée

2 celery sticks, sliced

1 fennel bulb, sliced

115 g/4 oz sliced mushrooms

225 g/8 oz tomatoes, sliced

1 tsp dark muscovado sugar

4 tbsp dried white breadcrumbs

salt and pepper

### TO SERVE

salad leaves

crusty bread

## METHOD

**1** Put the haricot beans in a large saucepan and add enough cold water to cover. Bring to the boil and continue to boil vigorously for 20 minutes. Drain, set aside and keep warm.

**2** Bring a large saucepan of lightly salted water to the boil. Add the penne and 1 tablespoon of the olive oil and cook for about 3 minutes. Drain the pasta, set aside and keep warm.

**3** Put the beans in a large, flameproof casserole. Add the vegetable stock and stir in the remaining oil, the onions, garlic, bay leaves, oregano, thyme, wine and tomato purée. Bring to the boil, then cover and cook in a preheated oven, 180°C/350°F/Gas Mark 4, for 2 hours.

**4** Add the penne, celery, fennel, mushrooms and tomatoes to the casserole and season to taste . Stir in the muscovado sugar and sprinkle over the breadcrumbs. Cover the dish and cook in the oven for 1 further hour.

**5** Serve hot with salad leaves and crusty bread.

# MEDITERRANEAN CHICKEN & PEPPERS

>Serves 4   >Preparation time: 5 minutes   >Cooking time: 35–40 minutes

## INGREDIENTS

8 skinless chicken thighs

2 tbsp wholemeal flour

2 tbsp olive oil

1 small onion, thinly sliced

1 garlic clove, crushed

1 each large red, yellow and green peppers, thinly sliced

400 g/14 oz canned chopped tomatoes

1 tbsp chopped fresh oregano, plus extra to garnish

salt and pepper

crusty wholemeal bread, to serve

## METHOD

**1** Toss the chicken thighs in the flour.

**2** Heat the oil in a wide pan and fry the chicken quickly until sealed and lightly browned, then remove from the pan. Add the onion to the pan and gently fry until soft. Add the garlic, peppers, tomatoes and oregano, then bring to the boil, stirring.

**3** Arrange the chicken over the vegetables, season well, then cover the pan tightly and simmer for 20–25 minutes, or until the chicken is tender and the juices run clear when the meat is pierced with a skewer.

**4** Season to taste, garnish with oregano and serve with crusty wholemeal bread.

# OVEN-BAKED RISOTTO

**>**Serves 4  **>**Preparation time: 10 minutes  **>**Cooking time: 50 minutes

## INGREDIENTS

4 tbsp olive oil

400 g/14 oz portobello or large field mushrooms, thickly sliced

115 g/4 oz pancetta or thick-cut smoked bacon, diced

1 large onion, finely chopped

2 garlic cloves, finely chopped

350 g/12 oz arborio or carnaroli rice

1.2 litres/2 pints chicken stock, simmering

2 tbsp chopped fresh tarragon or flat-leaved parsley

85 g/3 oz freshly grated Parmesan cheese, plus extra for sprinkling

salt and pepper

## METHOD

**1** Heat 2 tablespoons of the oil in a large, heavy-based frying pan over a high heat. Add the mushrooms and stir-fry for 2–3 minutes until golden. Transfer to a plate.

**2** Add the pancetta or bacon to the pan and cook for about 2 minutes, stirring frequently, until crisp and golden. Remove with a draining spoon and add to the mushrooms on the plate.

**3** Heat the remaining oil in a heavy-based saucepan over a medium heat. Add the onion and cook for about 2 minutes. Add the garlic and rice and cook, stirring, for about 2 minutes until the rice is well coated with the oil.

**4** Gradually stir the stock into the rice, then add the mushroom and pancetta or bacon mixture and the tarragon or parsley, and season with salt and pepper. Bring to the boil.

**5** Remove from the heat and transfer to a casserole dish.

**6** Cover and bake in a preheated oven, 180°C/350°F/Gas Mark 4, for about 20 minutes until the rice is almost tender and most of the liquid is absorbed. Uncover and stir in the Parmesan cheese. Bake for about 15 minutes longer until the rice is tender, but still firm to the bite. Serve hot with extra grated Parmesan for sprinkling.

# AZERBAIJANI LAMB PILAF

>Serves 4–6  >Preparation time: 5 minutes  >Cooking time: 45–55 minutes

## INGREDIENTS

2–3 tbsp olive oil

650 g/1 lb 7 oz boneless lamb shoulder, cut into 2.5 -m/1-inch cubes

2 onions, roughly chopped

1 tsp ground cumin

200 g/7 oz arborio, long-grain or basmati rice

1 tbsp tomato purée

1 tsp saffron threads

100 ml/3½ fl oz pomegranate juice

850 ml/1½ pints lamb or chicken stock, or water

115 g/4 oz dried apricots or prunes, ready soaked and halved

2 tbsp raisins

salt and pepper

4 tbsp mixed chopped fresh watercress and mint, to serve

## METHOD

**1** Heat the oil in a large flameproof casserole or wide saucepan over a high heat. Add the lamb in batches and cook for about 7 minutes, turning, until lightly browned all over.

**2** Add the onions to the casserole, reduce the heat to medium-high and cook for about 2 minutes, or until beginning to soften. Add the cumin and rice and cook for 2 minutes, stirring to coat well, until the rice becomes translucent. Stir in the tomato purée and saffron threads.

**3** Add the pomegranate juice and stock and bring the mixture to the boil, stirring once or twice. Stir the soaked apricots or prunes and the raisins into the casserole. Reduce the heat to low, cover, and simmer for 20–25 minutes, or until the lamb and rice are tender and the liquid has been absorbed.

**4** Sprinkle the chopped watercress and mint over the pilaf and serve straight from the pan.

# BEEF & POTATO GOULASH

›Serves 4   ›Preparation time: 15 minutes   ›Cooking time: 2¼ hours

## INGREDIENTS

2 tbsp vegetable oil

1 large onion, sliced

2 garlic cloves, crushed

750 g/1 lb 10 oz lean stewing steak

2 tbsp paprika

400 g/14 oz canned chopped tomatoes

2 tbsp tomato purée

1 large red pepper, deseeded and chopped

175 g/6 oz mushrooms, sliced

600 ml/1 pint beef stock

500 g/1 lb 2 oz potatoes, cut into large chunks

1 tbsp cornflour

salt and pepper

## TO GARNISH

4 tbsp low-fat natural yogurt

paprika

chopped fresh parsley

## METHOD

**1** Heat the oil in a large pan. Add the onion and garlic and cook over a medium heat, stirring occasionally, for 3–4 minutes until softened.

**2** Cut the steak into chunks, add to the pan and cook over a high heat for about 3 minutes until browned all over.

**3** Lower the heat to medium and stir in the paprika. Add the tomatoes, tomato purée, red pepper and mushrooms. Cook, stirring constantly, for 2 minutes.

**4** Pour in the stock. Bring to the boil, stirring occasionally, then reduce the heat to low. Cover and simmer gently for about 1½ hours until the meat is cooked through and tender.

**5** Add the potatoes, cover and cook for a further 20–30 minutes until tender.

**6** Blend the cornflour with a little water and add to the pan, stirring until thickened and blended. Cook for 1 minute then season with salt and pepper to taste. Top with the yogurt, sprinkle over the paprika and chopped fresh parsley and serve hot.

# LENTIL & RICE CASSEROLE

>Serves 4  >Preparation time: 5 minutes  >Cooking time: 40 minutes

## INGREDIENTS

225 g/8 oz red split lentils

50 g/1¾ oz long-grain white rice

1 litre/1¾ pints vegetable stock

150 ml/5 fl oz dry white wine

1 leek, cut into chunks

3 garlic cloves, crushed

400 g/14 oz canned chopped tomatoes

1 tsp ground cumin

1 tsp chilli powder

1 tsp garam masala

1 red pepper, deseeded and sliced

100 g/3½ oz small broccoli florets

8 baby corn cobs, halved lengthways

50 g/1¾ oz French beans, halved

1 tbsp shredded fresh basil

salt and pepper

fresh basil sprigs, to garnish

## METHOD

1 Place the lentils, rice, stock and wine in a flameproof casserole and cook over a gentle heat for 20 minutes, stirring occasionally.

2 Add the leek, garlic, tomatoes, cumin, chilli powder, garam masala, pepper, broccoli, corn cobs and French beans.

3 Bring the mixture to the boil, reduce the heat, cover and simmer for a further 10–15 minutes or until the vegetables are tender.

4 Add the shredded basil and season with salt and pepper to taste. Garnish with basil sprigs and serve.

# VEGETABLE JAMBALAYA

>Serves 4   >Preparation time: 10 minutes   >Cooking time: 50–55 minutes

## INGREDIENTS

75 g/2¼ oz brown rice

2 tbsp olive oil

2 garlic cloves, crushed

1 red onion, cut into eight pieces

1 aubergine, diced

1 green pepper, deseeded and diced

50 g/1¼ oz baby corn cobs, halved lengthways

50 g/1¼ oz frozen peas

100 g/3½ oz small broccoli florets

150 ml/5 floz vegetable stock

225 g/8 oz canned chopped tomatoes

1 tbsp tomato purée

1 tsp creole seasoning

½ tsp chilli flakes

salt and pepper

## METHOD

**1** Cook the rice in a saucepan of boiling water for 20 minutes or until cooked through. Drain and set aside.

**2** Heat the oil in a heavy-based frying pan. Add the crushed garlic and onion pieces and cook for 2–3 minutes, stirring.

**3** Add the aubergine, pepper, corn cobs, peas and broccoli to the pan and cook, stirring occasionally, for 2–3 minutes.

**4** Stir in the vegetable stock, tomatoes, tomato purée, creole seasoning and chilli flakes.

**5** Season to taste and cook over a low heat for 15–20 minutes, until the vegetables are tender.

**6** Stir the brown rice into the vegetable mixture and cook, mixing well, for 3–4 minutes or until hot. Transfer the vegetable jambalaya to warmed serving dishes and serve hot.

# POTATO & PASTA BAKE

›Serves 4  ›Preparation time: 15 minutes  ›Cooking time: 45 minutes

## INGREDIENTS

450 g/1 lb dried short-cut macaroni

1 tbsp olive oil

55 g/2 oz beef dripping

450 g/1 lb potatoes, thinly sliced

450 g/1 lb onions, sliced

225 g/8 oz mozzarella cheese, grated

150 ml/5 fl oz double cream

salt and pepper

crusty brown bread and butter, to serve

## METHOD

**1** Bring a large saucepan of lightly salted water to the boil. Add the macaroni and olive oil and cook for about 12 minutes, or until tender, but still firm to the bite. Drain the macaroni thoroughly and set aside.

**2** Melt the dripping in a large flameproof casserole, then remove from the heat.

**3** Make alternate layers of potatoes, onions, macaroni and grated cheese in the dish, seasoning well with salt and pepper between each layer and finishing with a layer of cheese on top. Finally, pour over the cream.

**4** Bake in a preheated oven, 200°C/400°F/Gas Mark 6, for 25 minutes. Remove the dish from the oven and carefully brown the top of the bake under a hot grill.

**5** Serve the bake straight from the dish with crusty brown bread and butter as a main course. Alternatively, serve as a vegetable accompaniment to your favourite main course.

# SEAFOOD RISOTTO WITH OREGANO

> Serves 4    > Preparation time: 10 minutes    > Cooking time: 25 minutes

## INGREDIENTS

1.2 litres/2 pints hot fish or chicken stock

350 g/12 oz arborio rice

3 tbsp butter

2 garlic cloves, chopped

250 g/9 oz mixed seafood, preferably raw, such as prawns, squid, mussels, clams and shrimps

2 tbsp chopped oregano, plus extra for garnishing

50 g/1¼ oz pecorino or Parmesan cheese, grated

## METHOD

1 In a large pan, bring the stock to the boil. Add the rice and cook for about 12 minutes, stirring, or until the rice is tender. Drain thoroughly, reserving any excess stock.

2 Heat the butter in a large frying pan and add the garlic, stirring.

3 Add the raw mixed seafood to the pan and cook for 5 minutes. If the seafood is already cooked, fry for 2–3 minutes.

4 Stir the oregano into the seafood mixture in the frying pan.

5 Add the cooked rice to the pan and cook for 2–3 minutes, stirring, or until hot. Add the reserved stock if the mixture gets too sticky.

6 Add the pecorino or Parmesan cheese and mix well.

7 Transfer the risotto to warmed serving dishes and serve hot.

# CHILLI CON CARNE

> Serves 4  > Preparation time: 10 minutes  > Cooking time: 2½ hours

## INGREDIENTS

750 g/1 lb 10 oz lean braising or stewing steak

2 tbsp vegetable oil

1 large onion, sliced

2–4 garlic cloves, crushed

1 tbsp plain flour

425 ml/15 fl oz tomato juice

400 g/14 oz canned chopped tomatoes

1–2 tbsp sweet chilli sauce

1 tsp ground cumin

425 g/15 oz canned red kidney beans, drained

½ tsp dried oregano

1–2 tbsp chopped fresh parsley

salt and pepper

chopped fresh herbs, to garnish

## TO SERVE

boiled rice

tortillas

## METHOD

**1** Cut the beef into 2-cm/¾-inch cubes. Heat the oil in a flameproof casserole and fry the beef cubes until well sealed. Remove the cubes from the casserole.

**2** Add the onion and crushed garlic to the casserole and cook until lightly browned. Stir in the flour and cook for 1–2 minutes. Stir in the tomato juice and tomatoes and bring to the boil. Add the beef and the chilli sauce, cumin and seasoning. Cover and place in a preheated oven, 160°C/325°F/Gas Mark 3, for 1½ hours or until almost tender.

**3** Stir in the kidney beans, oregano and chopped parsley and adjust the seasoning to taste. Cover the casserole and return to the oven for 45 minutes. Serve sprinkled with herbs, with boiled rice and tortillas.

# SAGE CHICKEN & RICE

>Serves 4  >Preparation time: 10 minutes  >Cooking time: 50 minutes

## INGREDIENTS

1 large onion, chopped

1 garlic clove, crushed

2 celery sticks, sliced

2 carrots, diced

2 sprigs fresh sage

300 ml/10 fl oz chicken stock

350 g/12 oz boneless, skinless chicken breasts

225 g/8 oz mixed brown and wild rice

400 g/14 oz canned chopped tomatoes

dash of Tabasco sauce

2 courgettes, trimmed and thinly sliced

100 g/3½ oz lean ham, diced

salt and pepper

fresh sage, to garnish

## TO SERVE

salad leaves

crusty bread

## METHOD

1 Place the onion, garlic, celery, carrots and sprigs of fresh sage in a large saucepan and pour in the chicken stock. Bring to the boil, cover the pan and simmer for 5 minutes.

2 Cut the chicken into 2.5-cm/1-inch cubes and stir into the pan with the vegetables. Cover the pan and cook for a further 5 minutes.

3 Stir in the mixed brown and wild rice and chopped tomatoes.

4 Add a dash of Tabasco sauce to taste and season well. Bring to the boil, cover and simmer for 25 minutes.

5 Stir in the sliced courgettes and diced ham and cook, uncovered, for 10 minutes, stirring occasionally, until the rice is just tender.

6 Remove the sprigs of fresh sage from the pan and discard. Season the dish, garnish with sage leaves and serve with plenty of salad leaves and fresh crusty bread.

# CHICKEN BIRYANI

> Serves 4  > Preparation time: 3½ hours  > Cooking time: 1½–1¾ hours

## INGREDIENTS

1½ tsp finely chopped fresh root ginger

1–2 garlic cloves, crushed

1 tbsp garam masala

1 tsp chilli powder

½ tsp ground turmeric

2 tsp salt

20 green/white cardamom seeds, crushed

300 ml/10 fl oz natural yogurt

1.5 kg/3 lb 5 oz chicken, skinned and cut into eight pieces

150 ml/5 fl oz milk

a few strands of saffron

6 tbsp ghee

2 medium onions, sliced

450 g/1 lb basmati rice

2 cinnamon sticks

4 black peppercorns

1 tsp black cumin seeds

4 green chillies

2 tbsp finely chopped fresh coriander leaves

4 tbsp lemon juice

## METHOD

1 Blend together the ginger, garlic, garam masala, chilli powder, turmeric, 1 teaspoon of the salt and the cardamom seeds and mix with the yogurt and chicken pieces. Set aside to marinate for 3 hours.

2 Pour the milk into a pan and bring to the boil. Pour it over the saffron and set aside.

3 Heat the ghee in a pan and cook the onions until golden brown. Remove half of the onions and ghee from the pan and set aside.

4 Place the rice, cinnamon sticks, peppercorns and black cumin seeds in a pan of water. Bring the rice to the boil and remove from the heat when half-cooked. Drain and place in a bowl. Mix in the remaining salt.

5 Add the chicken mixture to the pan with the onions and ghee. Deseed the chillies, if wished, and finely chop. Add half each of the chillies, coriander, lemon juice and saffron milk. Add the rice and then the rest of the ingredients, including the reserved fried onions and ghee. Cover tightly so no steam escapes. Cook on a low heat for 1–1¼ hours. Check that the meat is cooked through, mix thoroughly and serve.

# ITALIAN SAUSAGE CASSEROLE

>Serves 4  >Preparation time: 10 minutes  >Cooking time: 30 minutes

## INGREDIENTS

1 green pepper

8 Italian sausages

1 tbsp olive oil

1 large onion, chopped

2 garlic cloves, chopped

1 green pepper

225 g/8 oz fresh tomatoes, skinned and chopped, or 400 g/14 oz canned chopped tomatoes

2 tbsp sun-dried tomato paste

400 g/14 oz canned cannellini beans, drained

mashed potato or rice, to serve

## METHOD

1 Deseed the pepper and cut it into thin strips.

2 Prick the Italian sausages all over with a fork. Cook them under a preheated grill for 10–12 minutes, turning occasionally, until brown all over. Set aside and keep warm.

3 Heat the oil in a large frying pan. Add the onion, garlic and pepper to the frying pan and cook for 5 minutes, stirring occasionally, or until softened.

4 Add the tomatoes to the frying pan and simmer for 5 minutes, stirring occasionally, or until slightly reduced and thickened.

5 Stir the sun-dried tomato paste, cannellini beans and Italian sausages into the mixture in the frying pan. Cook for 4–5 minutes, or until the mixture is piping hot. Add 4–5 tablespoons of water, if the mixture becomes too dry during cooking.

6 Transfer the Italian sausage casserole to serving plates and serve with mashed potato or cooked rice.